D1219489

EARLY FLIGHT: 1900-1911

ORIGINAL PHOTOGRAPHS FROM THE
WRIGHT BROTHERS PERSONAL COLLECTION

Edited by
Ron Geibert and Tucker Malishenko

Landfall Press
Dayton, Ohio

EARLY FLIGHT: 1900-1911
Original Photographs from the Wright Brothers Personal Collection
Edited by Ron Geibert and Tucker Malishenko

ISBN-0-913428-38-8
Library of Congress Catalog Card No. 84-081339

All reproductions are exact size of the original photographs except Plates 19, 20, 29, 30, 40 and 50 which have been slightly reduced.

ACKNOWLEDGEMENT

We wish to thank Hamilton Standard Division of United Technologies Corporation and SITES for their generous support. Thanks also to the Friends of the Library at Wright State University and Dayton Newspapers, Inc. for helping make this book possible. Special thanks go to Wilkinson Wright for his enthusiastic encouragement and continued interest throughout the project. Most of all, we appreciate our wives for allowing us to "adopt" the Wright Brothers into our homes over the past year and a half.

Ron Geibert
Tucker Malishenko
Dayton, Ohio, May, 1984

FOREWORD

This publication augments an exhibition of vintage photographs from the Wright Brothers personal collection entitled *EARLY FLIGHT: 1900-1911*.

Curators for the exhibition and editors of this publication are Ron Geibert and Tucker Malishenko of Wright State University, Dayton, Ohio. Dr. Patrick Nolan, Wright State University Archivist, served as project director.

The exhibition opened at the U. S. Air Force Museum, Wright Patterson Air Force Base, Dayton, Ohio, in May, 1984.

EARLY FLIGHT: 1900-1911 is being circulated by the Smithsonian Institution Traveling Exhibition Service (SITES) in 1984-1986.

The National Air and Space Museum in Washington, D. C. is one of about 15 locations where the exhibit will be open to the public.

EARLY FLIGHT: 1900-1911

THE WRIGHT BROTHERS COLLECTION

by Patrick B. Nolan
Archivist, Wright State University

The airplane is perhaps the earliest great invention for which a complete written and photographic record exists. This record documents in word and picture every step and every experiment of the two brothers who together opened the door to the Age of Flight. Conscious of what they were achieving and determined to be recognized for their accomplishments, Orville and Wilbur Wright created a comprehensive archive of their efforts.

A close friend and some-time mentor, Octave Chanute, was deeply concerned that the Wrights would fail to gain recognition for their work. He feared they might be eclipsed by some later inventor unless they moved quickly to conclude a business deal for the sale of the airplane. In October of 1906 he wrote them:

"I cheerfully acknowledge that I have little idea how difficult the flying problem really is and that its solution is beyond my powers, but are you not too cocksure that yours is the only secret worth knowing and that others may not hit upon a solution in less than 'many times five years'? It took you much less than that and there are a few (very few) other able inventors in the world. The danger therefore is that others may achieve success . . . "[1]

In his calm, almost magisterial reply, Wilbur summed up his view of what he and his brother had achieved:

"If it were indeed true that others would be flying within a year or two, there would be reason in selling at any price but we are convinced that no one will be able to develop a practical flyer within five years. This opinion is based upon cold calculation. It takes into consideration practical and scientific difficulties whose existence is unknown to all but ourselves . . . When we see men laboring year after year on points we overcame in a few weeks, without ever getting far enough along to meet the worse points beyond, we know that their rivalry and competition are not to be feared for many years."[2]

The meticulously filed papers of the Wrights served them well. The notebooks and diaries enabled them to analyze their work, learn from their mistakes, and document each step in the inventive process. The photographs were intended both as visual records of flights, to show phenomena invisible to the pilot, and as illustrations for future articles and books which the brothers hoped to write.

Chanute urged them to keep a detailed photographic record: "Please take plenty of snapshots. You will want them to illustrate what you write."[3]

During the prolonged and acrimonious patent suits with Glenn Curtiss and others, the photographs and papers were invaluable in upholding the Wrights' 1906 patent application for their control methods.

After Wilbur's tragic and premature death in 1912, the complete files remained with Orville in his Dayton laboratory. On numerous occasions Orville began the task of writing the "definitive" account of their inventions but was unable to complete the effort. The archives were not made available to scholars and were only infrequently consulted by even the "authorized" biographer, Fred Kelly.[4]

The final disposition of the papers was left unclear at the time of Orville's death in 1948. His will stated that the executors should select whatever institution or institutions they deemed proper to receive the materials. At that time there was no archive or library in Dayton prepared to house the collection properly, and the decision was made to divide

11

the files. Somewhat over half the items were donated to the Library of Congress in 1949.[5]

The Library of Congress selected some 100 printed items to supplement their own holdings in aeronautics, 303 glass-plate negatives of Wright Brothers photographs, and the majority of the notebooks, journals and correspondence of the brothers. All of the remaining papers were kept by the Wright heirs and were housed in the Dayton home of Mrs. Ivonette Wright Miller, daughter of Lorin Wright and niece of Wilbur and Orville.

The Millers, as well as the other Wright heirs, wanted the papers to remain in the Dayton area, in a repository conducive to research and exhibit. In 1975 the collection was donated to Wright State University.

It is truly fitting that the newest state university in Ohio be the repository for this collection because from its beginning Wright State was conceived as a living memorial to the achievements of the Wright Brothers. Named in their honor, founded in 1964 as the Dayton campus of Miami University and The Ohio State University, Wright State University became a separate institution in 1967.

It was built on land deeded in part by Wright Patterson Air Force Base and lies within a mile of Huffman Prairie, the site of Simms Station, where the Wrights perfected their flying machines in 1904 and 1905. The memorial to them on Wright Brothers Hill is adjacent to the campus, and the U.S. Air Force Museum, which commemorates the history of flight, is nearby.

The University today is proud of the Wright Brothers collection and around that nucleus has built a growing archive on aviation history. The Wright Brothers Collection numbers over 6000 items.

Included are more than 200 technical books, journals and pamphlets which constituted the Wrights' research library and extensive files of their business, legal and financial records.[6] Manuscript diaries of their father, Bishop Milton Wright, virtually continuous from 1857 to 1917, give an unparalleled view of his career and interests as well as the activities of his famous sons.

Perhaps the most valuable portion of the Collection are the photograph files. From a collection of 3500 photographs there are over 1500 original prints of the Wright Brothers' aviation experiments and demonstration flights. Virtually all of the photos from 1900 to 1905 were made by Wilbur and Orville from their own glass-plate negatives in their home photo lab. A significant number of the glass plates now at the Library of Congress were under water during the Dayton flood of 1913 and severely damaged. The prints at Wright State were made from the negatives prior to their damage in the flood and are the best surviving images. Many of these photographs are unique, with no other known existing copy.

In addition to the documentation on early flights in the United States, the Collection is particularly rich in photographs of the Wrights' European flights. Wilbur's flights in France at Le Mans in 1908 and Pau in 1909, and in Italy near Rome are fully covered. Perhaps the most outstanding images are of Orville's flights at Tempelhof Field, outside of Berlin in 1909. Many of these pictures are artistically as well as historically noteworthy.

The fifty-six prints illustrated in this book were originally selected for public exhibition in a show titled "Early Flight: 1900-1911, Original Photographs from the Wright Brothers Personal Collection." The choice of prints was made by the curators after carefully weighing the historical and aesthetic contents of the images, their physical condition, and the informational and evidential values of the photographs.

With the strong support of Mr. Wilkinson Wright, a great-nephew of the brothers, funding was received from the Hamilton Standard Division of United Technologies Corporation. The Friends of the Wright State University Library lent invaluable assistance in mounting the exhibit and serving as the grant administrative office.

From 1899 to 1903, an astonishingly brief period, Wilbur and Orville Wright "invented" the airplane. Their work during this time has been described by Dr. Malcolm Ritchie:

"Between May 30, 1899 and December 18, 1903, they not only taught themselves aeronautical engineering, aerodynamics, and test flying, they also designed and built a series of increasingly sophisticated machines: a controllable 5-foot biplane kite, three large gliders, three aerodynamic test machines, one airplane, a complete airplane control system, one engine, and two propellers (for which they had first to develop a propeller theory)."[7]

During this period, while their wind-tunnel research was done in Dayton, all their flying was accomplished on the sand dunes of Kill Devil Hills at Kitty Hawk, North Carolina.

In 1904 and 1905 the brothers perfected their skills as pilots and turned the first Wright Flyer from an experimental vehicle into the world's first practical airplane, capable of fully-controlled flight. This epoch-making work took place at Huffman Prairie (also called Simms Station) a pasture some ten miles east of Dayton.

The Wrights retired from active piloting for almost three years, 1906-1908, while they concentrated on negotiating their contracts for sale of the Flyer, establishing companies for marketing the plane in America and Europe, and obtaining the final patent for their control system from the U.S. Patent Office. It was during this fallow period that Chanute, as quoted earlier, urged them to sell before they were surpassed by other inventors.

Beginning in 1908, the Wrights embarked upon the most glamorous and exciting portion of their career. They went to Europe to demonstrate the Flyer publicly and to show the world what they had accomplished.

They first returned to Kitty Hawk, May 6-14, 1908, to hone their rusty flying skills. After practicing at Kitty Hawk, Wilbur sailed for France and astonished spectators with his ability to perform figure-8's, circles and other maneuvers while French pilots had barely been able to hop a short distance in a straight line.

From August 8 to August 13, 1908 at Hunaudieres Race Course, near Le Mans and then from Le Mans, Wilbur continued to demonstrate his skills and to train French student pilots in the operation of the Flyer.

Simultaneously with Wilbur's departing for France, Orville left Dayton for Washington, D.C. He intended to conduct acceptance tests with the Wright airplane for the U.S. Army Signal Corps. His flights, made at Fort Myer, Virginia, near Arlington, were spectacularly successful until on September 17, 1908 disaster struck.

One of the propellers split, causing the plane to crash. Orville's passenger, Lt. Thomas E. Selfridge was killed (the first fatality in an airplane crash) and Orville seriously injured.

In 1909 the brothers continued to gain fame and recognition for their flights. Orville, still recovering from his injuries, joined Wilbur in the resort town of Pau at the foot of the Pyrenees. At Pont-Long Flying Field, from February 3 to March 20, 1909 many flights were made which focused the world's attention on the small city.

From France, Wilbur and Orville went to Italy and Wilbur trained several Italian student pilots at Rome. At Centocelle Flying Field, from April 15 to April 27, 1909, he flew before Italian royalty and large crowds of spectators.

Orville returned to the United States during the summer of 1909 to resume his aborted trials of the Army airplane at Fort Myers. On the last day of these flights he satisfied the government speed requirement and earned a $5000 bonus by flying at 42.5 miles per hour.

The Wrights' last European flights were in Germany at two locations, Tempelhof Field outside Berlin and Bornstedt Field near Potsdam. Orville, fresh from his triumph at Fort Myer, again demonstrated his uncanny skill as a pilot before huge crowds and the Kaiser himself between August 30 and October 15, 1909.

The Wrights ended their flying exhibits in the United States, with flights at air shows in New York, Alabama and many other locations. The Wright Company factory in Dayton was the scene of great activity as planes were manufactured for sale at home and abroad. However, the good times soon came to an end.

After Wilbur's early death from typhoid fever in 1912, Orville began to retire from the aviation business. In 1916 he severed his ties with the Wright Company and on May 13, 1918 made his last flight as a pilot.

An era in aviation history had come to an end.

Perhaps their father, Bishop Milton Wright, described the work of the two brothers best. Responding to the perennial question of which brother contributed the most and was the leader of the partnership, the Bishop replied:

"Wilbur in every respect was uncommon in his intellect and attainments - was a surprise to those near him. But he seemed not to care for notice. Orville's mind grew steadily, and in invention he was fully equal to his brother. They are equal in their inventions, neither claiming any superiority above the other, nor accepting any honor to the neglect of the other."[8]

NOTES

[1]Octave Chanute to Wilbur Wright, October 15, 1906, in Marvin W. McFarland, ed., *The Papers of Wilbur and Orville Wright* (N.Y.: Arno Press, 1972). Vol. II, pp. 730-731.

[2]Wilbur Wright to Octave Chanute, October 10 and 28, 1906, in McFarland, ed., *The Papers of Wilbur and Orville Wright,* Vol. II, pp. 729-732.

[3]Octave Chanute to Wilbur Wright, August 19, 1901, in McFarland, ed., *The Papers of Wilbur and Orville Wright,* Vol. I, p.83.

[4]Fred C. Kelly, *The Wright Brothers. A Biography Authorized by Orville Wright* (N.Y.: Harcourt, Brace & Co., 1943).

[5]The particulars are fully described by Marvin W. McFarland and Arthur Renstrom in the *Library of Congress Quarterly Journal of Current Acquisitions,* 7: 22-34 (August 1950).

[6]See Patrick B. Nolan and John A. Zamonski, *The Wright Brothers Collection: A Guide to the Technical, Business and Legal, Genealogical, Photographic and Other Archives at Wright State University* (N. Y.: Garland Publishing, 1977).

[7]Malcolm L. Ritchie, "The Research and Development Methods of Wilbur and Orville Wright", *Astronautics and Aeronautics,* July-August, 1978, pp. 56-67.

[8]Bishop Milton Wright, manuscript sketch dated 1916, *Wright Brothers Collection,* MS-1, Box 8, File 8, Department of Archives and Special Collections, Wright State University Library, Dayton, Ohio.

DAMNED IF THEY AIN'T FLEW

by Ron Geibert

"There's one thing all of us want to do . . . to get up in the air. In my sleep I can fly . . . I fly all of the time. I can't get enough of it."

Jacques Henri-Lartigue
photographer, age 12,
Rouzat, France, 1906[1]

Returning from a six-week trip to the sand dunes of Kitty Hawk, North Carolina, in 1901, two bicycle manufacturers from Dayton, Ohio, retreated to the darkroom in a wooden shed behind their home.

Processing exposed glass dry plates in a set of ruby-colored trays, they would "pass moments of as thrilling interest as any in the field, when the image begins to appear on the plate and it is yet an open question whether we have a picture of a flying machine, or merely a patch of open sky."[2]

Wilbur and Orville Wright, self-taught as photographers, would then contact print the negatives, often laboring over the sink with a child from the neighborhood standing alongside.

Family members, relatives and friends often participated in and enjoyed the photographs made by the Wright brothers. They used a 4 x 5 inch format camera to provide a visual diary of their work and recreation.

Friends would gather about the large dining room table at 7 Hawthorn Street, passing around newly-made photographs of neighborhood children, the bicycle shop, holidays and parties, local landscapes and newsworthy events (a fire, train wreck or flood).

The aesthetic improvement of the photographs from year to year was apparent as the brothers, sharing the camera, moved from static and centered subject matter to more innovatively composed images incorporating the entire frame and the foreground to background space.

Camping excursions and their Dayton neighborhood provided countless opportunities to challenge their artistic and technical expertise. One example is *Wilbur Wright at Pinnacles near Dayton, Ohio, 1898.*[3]

This photograph, in which a towering structure shadows Wilbur, is remarkably similar to many of the survey photographs of the 1860's and the 1870's by the famous landscape photographer William Jackson. The contrast of the diminutive figure with the rough terrain places the work within the context of one 19th Century attitude toward nature—the tenuous position of man on the land.

Other landscape photographs made by the brothers at the same time present yet another attitude toward the landscape—one of romantic reverence.

Another photograph entitled *Katharine Wright, Harriet Silliman and Agnes Osborn in carriage in front of 7 Hawthorn Street,*[4] circa 1900, demonstrates an improved control of the materials, as evidenced by the broader tonal scale and new compositional devices such as the balanced placement of the tree and the abbreviated carriage and horse.

Photography was undergoing a technological and aesthetic revolution when Wilbur and Orville pursued it as a hobby in the late 1890's and as a scientific tool and expressive medium in the early 1900's. The slow and arduous collodion wet-plate process, a system that required the photographer to polish, coat, sensitize and develop the glass plate on the spot, had been replaced by more sensitive and convenient gelatin bromide dry plates. The Wrights' requirement of short exposures to negate motion demanded the latest in this dry plate technology.[5]

Improved and new films, such as non-halation emulsions with their increased sensitivity, allowed the brothers to make "instantaneous" photographs of their plane against the brilliant sky and reflective sands.[6] By today's standards the films were painfully slow, with outdoor exposures rarely shorter than $\frac{1}{25}$ of a second and often of one second duration.

Photographing interiors was even more difficult, with exposures stretching in excess of one minute. This exposure time could be drastically shortened by the use of a blinding magnesium powder flash (Plate 17).

Using photography as a documentary tool and as a visual interpretation of their experiments, the brothers wanted the clear and precise images that were only possible with a large view camera. During their trips to Kitty Hawk between 1900 and 1911, they used two different camera formats, a 4 x 5 inch in 1900 and 1901 and a 5 x 7 inch from 1902 on. Although improvements were also being made in the newly introduced roll films, the large negatives still provided superior grain structure and sharpness when contact printed.

The larger 5 x 7 inch wooden camera, a Korona, was purchased from the Gundlach Optical Company of Rochester, N. Y. This progressive company was founded by Ernst Gundlach, an immigrant from Berlin and a former optical designer at Bausch and Lomb.[7]

The addition of a convertible anastigmat lens allowed the brothers to vary the focal length from a wide angle to a long lens.[8] A combination that provided a slightly wide angle view was most often used as it increased the probability of the craft being captured on the photographic plate and gave a better sense of the place. A pneumatic shutter, film holders, focusing cloth and case completed the outfit.

Much of the time during the Wrights' first visit to Kitty

Hawk in 1900 was spent in photographing the surroundings. Nearly all of the surviving negatives of this trip are landscape photographs and views of their camp.

Since the site had been recommended by the U. S. Weather Bureau as conducive to glider experimentation, Wilbur and Orville had come with high expectations. They must have been mildly surprised at the barrenness of the land; only a few twisted and wind-swept trees broke up the constantly shifting horizon.

In a letter to their friend Octave Chanute, Wilbur wrote: "To the north, northeast, east and southeast there is nothing but flat plain and ocean for a thousand miles nearly. It is an ideal place for gliding experiments except for its inaccessibility. The person who goes there . . . cannot depend on getting any needed article from the outside world in less than three weeks."[9]

Venturing out from their tent, they recorded the surf, sand and campground from many viewpoints. They also photographed local residents. The few people of Kitty Hawk, living in virtual isolation, must have been fascinated or skeptical, or both, when asked to pose.

The most striking of this group of pictures is a small portrait of great intensity entitled *Life Saving Crew, Kill Devil Hill Life Saving Station, Kitty Hawk, 1900* (Plate 3). Interestingly, another shot of the group, without the variety of head postures and eye contact, lacks the intimacy and directness of the negative Wilbur and Orville chose to print.

The Wrights' experience in photographing groups of people during the previous years in Dayton paid off handsomely in this instance. Whereas the portrait excelled in its directness, most of the other photographs taken of the land and glider displayed in comparison a timidity in the new environment.

Their attention was devoted almost exclusively to glider experimentation during their second trip in 1901. A topographical survey in photographs was made of Big Kill Devil Hill, the highest of three launching sites near their camp, and these photographs suggest the countless struggles up the hill that were to follow.

Dwarfed by the upended glider (Plate 7), Orville posed for Wilbur, providing a reference of scale. More confident of their calculations with the passing year, the brothers began their estimated 50 to 100 glides with exuberance amid the heat and swarms of mosquitoes.

In their 1900 experiments, when the glider/kite was controlled by tether lines, they had a relatively stable subject (Plate 1). The next year, though, the free glides complicated matters. The angle of descent and the speed with which the glider dropped were unpredictable.

The most difficult problem for the photographer was simply to catch the soaring craft within the frame. And working with a cumbersome camera on a tripod, there was time only to make one exposure per glide. With this limitation, both brothers were forced to trust their instincts of timing, to learn the field view of the lens and to work intuitively in contrast to their usual calculated, scientific approach.

Arriving at a successful combination of Wilbur's "precise approach" and Orville's "bubbling over with ideas and dreams"[10] would make the following fall their most innovative and rewarding period of photography.

The grace and austerity in composition that the brothers began to exercise in 1902 is exemplified in the photograph *Orville Wright skimming the ground, Kitty Hawk, October 10, 1902* (Plate 10). The harmony of motion and form between the glider and the overlapping dunes is eloquent in the small mauve colored print.

Nearly all of the approximately dozen other existing negatives of glider flights from this year exhibit the same handling and refinement in camera framing and use of delicate lines and shapes. Although each test glide carried real danger and uncertainty with it — and photographing them certainly involved a degree of luck — the repetitive flights honed the skills of the pilot and photographer alike. Trampling the moonlike landscape (Plate 12) for a better vantage point and making some glides for the purpose of taking photographs, the brothers made enchanting, yet frank images of the events and the location.

When the smaller hand held cameras such as the Kodak

enraptured the public and saturated society with "photographers" in the 1890's and early 1900's, the magical aura surrounding the camera operator was removed. To counter this loss of status, many professional and amateur photographers disregarded the unique qualities of their medium (incredible amount of detail, long tonal range, etc.) and turned to manipulation of the negative and/or print until it resembled a painting. This alteration of the characteristics of a photograph, often combined with allegorical or slightly soft-focused subject matter, was part of a movement known as Pictorialism.

In contrast, the Wrights' scientific genius and aesthetic perception allowed them to make photographs contrary to the prevalent trends in "artistic" photography. Their fusion of straightforward documentation with a purity of photographic techniques was concurrent with the reawakening of straight photography that was taking place in part of the photographic community during this period.

Indeed, the photographs of the Wrights suggested the same ideals and spirit that Alfred Stieglitz[11] and others were coming to realize and expound at this time in New York City: the recognition that the camera had its own set of aesthetics and needed to be free from the domination of painting.

Interested in craftmanship and ignorant of political struggles and trends in the art world, Wilbur and Orville were producing images which were satisfying on both scientific and aesthetic grounds. They were, obviously enough, *not* producing the "villainous commercial trash, or . . . cheap arty stuff"[12] that Stieglitz railed against.

If the brothers can be faulted in their photographic work at Kitty Hawk, it would be for the unevenness of their print quality. The early years (1900-1901) are represented often by drastically cropped prints, some only a few square inches in size, now in various states of fading and yellowing. Chemically stained from uneven and shortened processing, the prints are now probably no better or worse than when they were so hastily made by the brothers.

From 1902 on, the print quality was still occasionally rough, but it improved immeasurably. Using the larger 5 x 7 camera evoked an air of "seriousness" to their camera ven-

tures. As the brothers approached their goal of powered, controlled flight, photography became a more essential ingredient of their work. They became much more consistent in their use of the whole negative in framing, taking advantage of the large negative size to record the scene with clarity and accuracy.

Despite the harsh and contrasty light reflected off the sand at Kitty Hawk, the prints made by the brothers often exhibit the beautiful and subtle tonal gradations that are possible in a photographic print. In their Dayton darkroom, Wilbur and Orville would customarily make two or more contact prints from each negative for publication purposes and to keep up with their proud father's urge to mail copies off to relatives and friends.

"Damned if they ain't flew!"[13] could be a more colorful title for *First Flight, 10:35 AM, December 17, 1903* (Plate 18). The fact that this is one of the most widely published photographs in history demonstrates our fascination with the ability to escape the grip of the earth, if even for a scant twelve seconds.

We can only speculate as to the brothers' thoughts as Orville positioned, focused and preset the camera yet another time. Occasionally the significance or difficulty of an event demanded the attention of both brothers and required that an assistant or visitor actually operate the camera shutter (Plates 4, 5, 11 and 18). Attempting the first powered flight was certainly one of those events!

The role of camera operator for the historic moment was delegated to John T. Daniels, a member of the Kill Devil Hill life saving crew. Carefully following Orville's instructions, he released the shutter as the plane lifted from the launching rail, with Orville lying prone on the plane and Wilbur running alongside.

There could be no doubt among the observers that powered flight had been achieved and that *this* negative would *not* have a patch of open sky!

Wilbur and Orville continued to photograph after that eventful December day in 1903. During 1904 and 1905 they set up camp at Huffman Prairie, farmland located on the eastern outskirts of Dayton. Here they perfected the first practical airplane. Often in view of passengers on the nearby interurban trolley, they would fly controlled circles and figure 8's with increasing speeds and altitudes. Flights in excess of 30 minutes gave them ample opportunities to make pictures.

Unfortunately, most of the photographs made at Huffman Prairie during this two year period are missing the gestural qualities and expressive use of light so characteristic of the earlier photographic work at Kitty Hawk and thus are ordinarily tame in both execution and concept. We can only speculate as to the reasons.

Perhaps the familiarity with the local setting — without the levels of viewpoint that the shifting dunes at Kitty Hawk provided — dampened creative energies. More likely the uniformity and regularity of the flights made documentation less significant. Possibly the Wrights felt that their "proof" now rested in a craft that could verify their claims in a far more convincing manner than any piece of paper.

For whatever reasons, their interest in photography began to wane. However, there were beautiful exceptions within the decline. A noteworthy example is *Flight 46, Simms Station, October 4, 1905* (Plate 19).

Shifting from his usual horizontal to a vertical framing, Wilbur captured the energy and speed of the fabric-covered craft as it loomed over his shoulder into the view of the camera. The slightly askew horizon line and the blur of the plane give the image an improvised and authentic look. This photograph equals in design and intensity the gliding photographs of 1902 and the first flight image of 1903.

One or both of the brothers returned to Kitty Hawk twice after their 1903 success, before patent defenses, business concerns and Wilbur's premature death in 1912 disrupted their work. In 1908, both went back to Kill Devil Hill for flying practice, and in 1911 Orville made a series of record-setting glides there.

The gaps in their photographic activities (1906-1907, 1909) did not interfere with their making dynamic pictures during both these visits. They returned to a wind and scavanger damaged hangar that was haunting in its ravaged state (Plates 21, 56). With the carcass of the 1902 glider partially concealed beneath the sands, or the tenuously supported hangar door revealing discarded and sun bleached woodscraps, the photographer became an elegist, singing a song of desolation and, at the same time, suggesting the mythological phoenix.

Flight has always held a special fascination for Europeans. The sky had been invaded in Paris 125 years earlier (1783) by two French "aeronauts" aboard a hot air balloon designed by the Montgolfier brothers.

In the following centuries, the desire to fly infected people of all backgrounds and ages, including Jacques Henri-Lartigue, a child gifted with special artistic talents and recognized today for his work in the "snapshot" genre. Lartigue wrote in his diary: "We have many adventures at the Chateau de Rouzat with the giant kites Zissou (his brother Maurice's nickname) built with the help of Papa. I see them soar up to meet the clouds; it almost makes me dizzy to breathe in the air that makes them rise up so high, so high . . . "[14]

Along with many other Frenchmen, Lartigue had followed and photographed the exploits of Gabriel Voisin and others as they attempted to match the published successes of the two young Americans, Wilbur and Orville Wright. French aviators tried to make copies of the 1902 Wright glider from photographs used in a Paris lecture in 1903 by Octave Chanute, an early aviation pioneer and friend of the Wrights.

Failing to grasp the principles of wing-warping and the interlocking between the warp and the rudder, these French efforts mostly met with failure.

By 1908, smug with a few successful "hops" and short distance flights, they were quite unprepared for the incredible performances of the quiet-spoken Ohioans who came to demonstrate in France, Italy and Germany.

Any remaining skepticism that the Americans' claims were valid was shattered with the words "Il vole, Il vole!" (he flies, he flies)[15] when Wilbur took his flyer above the race course near Le Mans, France in 1908.

Of those August, 1908 days Wilbur wrote to Orville that "the newspapers and the French aviators nearly went wild with the excitement. Bleriot and Delagrange were so excited they could scarcely speak, and Kapferer could only gasp

19

and could not talk at all. You would have almost died of laughter if you could have seen them."[16] In another letter to Orville, he described one crowd of spectators with the words "princes and millionaires are as thick as fleas."[17]

At the public demonstrations in Pau, Rome and Berlin in 1909, the crowds sometimes numbered in the hundreds of thousands. The brothers' advanced flyer, now able to carry aloft a passenger, had royalty and the famous vying to be asked to accompany Wilbur or Orville.

At least one of these flights met with an unexpected result. Mrs. Hart O. Berg, wife of the Wrights' European business manager, tied the bottom of her skirt and coat closed prior to a flight as a safety and moral precaution. After the flight, when she walked away in tiny steps, skirt and coat still tied, a dress designer present took note and soon after the hobble skirt was the rage of the fashionable.[18]

The large numbers of professional and amateur photographers at the public demonstrations in Europe and later in America made it less crucial for the Wrights to make their own photographs.[19] Nevertheless, they were careful to acquire photographs made by others.

In addition to its documentation of flight, the collection of prints that they gathered in 1908 and 1909 is fascinating in its overview of both technical and aesthetic developments in photography of the time.

As the collection shows, the roll film and small plate cameras, some selling for only one dollar, had nearly taken over the photographic market. Kodak Brownie and Folding Pocket cameras and German "Klapp" or strut cameras gave the photographer a more mobile and rapidly working instrument. With the spontaneity in handling that the smaller camera allowed came many distinctive traits that we associate with the snapshot.

Truncated bodies, a temporal quality and looser compositional structure became part of the photographic repertoire (Plate 31). Everyone could make his own personal notations of what he saw and felt. Later the images could be sorted and arranged in albums with written identification or anecdotes added.

In one curious example from the collection (Plate 48), one photographer went to the point of even inking an "X" directly onto the negative, therefore printing a white mark to draw attention to a spot of significance. Inclusion of friends or relatives in the scene — or even oneself by asking a nearby stranger to press the button — gave real proof that the photographer was there (Plates 32-35).

Photographs with vitality and visual richness resulted from such techniques as panning the camera with the moving object to freeze it against a blurred background (Plates 32, 36) or by unconventional points of view (Plate 46).

These new visual possibilities with the smaller cameras are nowhere better illustrated in the collection than with the photograph entitled *Man with camera watching Wilbur Wright fly past, Pau, France, 1909* (Plate 28). The photographer, one J. Callizo, captured within his frame a photographer attempting to do what he had already accomplished; to make an exposure of the the same rapidly moving flyer. This image, along with others in the collection likely made by Callizo (i.e. Plate 29), demonstrate how one talented photographer, with a feeling for space and design, approached the incredible events.

In 1909, the Wrights contracted to provide a demonstration in Berlin at Tempelhof Field for the newspaper *Lokal-Anzeiger*. The owner, August Scherl (or one of his photographers), produced a record of unparalleled completeness (Plates 37-47). The meticulously made prints give evidence of another photographer actively involved with the new freedoms allowed by the new hand-held cameras.

A sense of place and contact with the observers, combined with compositional elegance by the use of diagonals, gives life to the images. *Crowds running to watch flight at Tempelhof, Germany, 1909* (Plate 47) is magnificent in the exhilaration and animation that it expresses.

As in France and Italy, crowds gathered, dressed in their finest apparel, to witness one of the miracles of the day. Vendors sold refreshments (Plate 37) or postcards of early aviation personalities.[20] From photographs of the roped-off crowds and helmeted patrols, to the airplane being guarded in its temporary quarters, Scherl presented to Wilbur and Orville unquestionably one of the most beautiful and outstanding groups of early flight photographs in the world.

Not all of the photographers who donated prints to the brothers at this time were quite as precise as Scherl in providing accurate descriptions of the Wrights' flights. On more than one occasion photographers,[21] using darkroom "magic," combined two different negatives into one print.

Probably as a clever commemorative piece, one photographer printed the silhouette of a Wright Flyer over the Dayton skyline (Plate 51). Most likely the event was the Dayton Homecoming Celebration of 1909, when the flag bedecked city turned out to welcome the brothers home. The crowds even lined the roof-tops. Lest any unsuspecting individual grant authenticity to the print, however, Orville in his own handwriting labeled it "Fake" on the front and back surfaces.

Accuracy always played a crucial role in the Wrights' experimentation, from the compiling of data from a wind tunnel apparatus (Plate 9) to the actual flights in the field. It seems appropriate then, that a descriptive process such as photography became a part of their work.

Much of the public was familiar with the social commentary photography of Jacob Riis and Lewis Hine, the war reportage of Matthew Brady and Alexander Gardner and the lyrical impressionism of Edward Steichen. Unfortunately, other than a published print here or there, it did not have access to the Wrights' eloquent and elegant images.

In their photography Wilbur and Orville illustrate the view of the French art historian Pierre Francastel that "only artists and scientists see around them new groupings of phenomena; and they alone express them in transmissible terms capable of development. There is no contradiction between the evolution of science and art and the evolution of modern technique."[22]

The Wrights, primarily engineers and scientists, found in photography another outlet for their creative energy. In spite of the countless headaches and distractions that making photographs must have provided in the field, the brothers shared the roles of documentarian and visual interpreter between them, as they so uniquely shared everything in their lives.

In doing so, they provided a rare opportunity for posterity to share not only the product of their technical genius — the miracle of powered flight — but also the process by which that miracle was achieved. This documentation itself now provides rare insight into their own unique amalgamation of science and art.

In the classical myth, Icarus fell to earth when he dared to fly too close to the sun with his feather and wax wings. In 1901, in a moment of frustration and despair, Wilbur said that man would not fly within a thousand years.[23] But within two years this negative prophesy proved wrong.

In 1903, the same sun that sent Icarus to his death provided the light that etched onto a silver-coated glass plate the image of Wilbur himself watching his brother fly past him on fabric covered wings.

NOTES

[1]Jacques Henri-Lartigue, *Diary of a Century,* ed. Richard Avedon (N.Y.: Viking Press, 1970), unnumbered page.

[2]Wilbur Wright, "Some Aeronautical Experiments," lecture presented to the Western Society of Engineers, Chicago, Illinois, September 18, 1901. Published in the Society's *Journal,* December, 1901. (reprint) p. 21.

[3]Photograph LC-W85-46, Prints and Photographs Division, Library of Congress, Washington, D.C.

[4]Ibid., LC-US262-66293

[5]The notebooks kept by the Wrights record that they used orthochromatic, non-halation, Stanley (Newton, Mass.), and Cramer (St. Louis) photographic plates. Marvin W. McFarland, editor, *The Papers of Wilbur and Orville Wright: Vol. 1* (N.Y.: McGraw Hill Book Co., 1953, reprinted in 1972 by Arno Press, N.Y.), p. 255.

[6]The shutter used by the Wrights, in addition to having settings of $\frac{1}{50}$, ¼, ½, 1 and 2, had selections of T, B and I (Time, Bulb and Instantaneous). The brothers most often used the I setting which was probably about $\frac{1}{25}$ of a second in duration.

[7]Reese V. Jenkins, *Images and Enterprise: Technology and the American Photographic Industry, 1839-1925* (Baltimore: Johns Hopkins University Press, 1976), p. 214.

[8]The convertible lens consisted of elements 18 ", 12 " and 10 " in length. The $^{18}/_{12}$ combination used most often had a focal length of 7 ½ inches and a maximum aperture of f/7.5.

[9]McFarland, *Vol. 1,* p. 40.

[10]Unpublished interviews with Ivonette Wright Miller, Kettering, Ohio, December 15, 1983, and Horace Wright, Bellbrook, Ohio, December 19, 1983.

[11]Alfred Stieglitz was instrumental in bringing about the acceptance of photography as a fine art and introducing "modern art" onto the American scene.

[12]Thomas Craven, "Stieglitz— Old Master of the Camera," *Saturday Evening Post,* 216 (January 8, 1944), p. 15.

[13]Statement made by a member of the Kill Devil Hill Life Saving crew on December 17, 1903. Valerie Moolman, *The Road to Kitty Hawk* (Alexandria, Virginia: Time-Life Books, 1980), p. 153.

[14]Lartigue, *Diary of a Century,* unnumbered page.

[15]Exclamation of 13-year-old Henri Delgove and a friend on witnessing the August 8, 1908 flight near Le Mans, as told to author Harry Combs, *Kill Devil Hill* (Boston: Houghton Mifflin Company, 1979), p. 281.

[16]McFarland, *Vol. 2,* p. 912.

[17]Combs, p. 315.

[18]Fred C. Kelly, *The Wright Brothers* (N.Y.: Harcourt, Brace and Co., 1943), p. 247. (Katharine Wright, sister of Wilbur and Orville, is in a similar state of restraint in Plate 29.)

[19]Orville gave up using the 5 x 7 view camera for aviation photographs after Wilbur's death. The camera was stored until the early 1930's when Orville gave it to his nephew Horace Wright, also an avid amateur photographer. The view camera miraculously survived the 1974 Xenia, Ohio tornado and is now on loan to Carillon Park, Dayton, Ohio. For most of the remainder of his life, Orville made personal photographs with a much smaller hand-held camera, a German-designed Goertz. Horace Wright interview.

[20]The face of Count Ferdinand von Zeppelin is on flags and postcards in the collection photograph 18-9-50, Wright Brothers Collection, M S-1, Archives and Special Collections, Wright State University, Dayton, Ohio.

[21]Aviation historian Charles H. Gibbs-Smith has determined that another photograph of the Wrights in actuality is a composite print. Arthur G. Renstrom, *Wilbur and Orville Wright: Pictorial Materials,* (Washington, D. C., The Library of Congress, 1982), p. 95.

[22]Pierre Francastel quoted by Jean-Luc Daval, *Photography, History of an Art* (N. Y.: Rizzoli International Publications, Inc., 1982), p. 11.

[23]Kelly, p. 75.

KITTY HAWK, 1900
To the north, northeast, east and southeast there is nothing but flat plain and ocean for a thousand miles nearly. It is an ideal place for gliding experiments except for its inaccessibility. The person who goes there . . . cannot depend on getting any needed article from the outside in less than three weeks.

Wilbur Wright to aeronaut Octave Chanute, Nov. 16, 1900

PLATE 1 — Tethered glider flown as a kite, Kitty Hawk, 1900. Glider No. 1 had wing span of 17 feet. Wright photo

PLATE 2 — Wilbur scouring pans at Kitty Hawk, 1900. Orville did the cooking.
Wright photo

PLATE 3 — Crew of the Kill Devil Hill Lifesaving Station, Kitty Hawk, 1900. They often helped. Wright photo

30

PLATE 4 — Friend and advisor, Octave Chanute at Kitty Hawk in 1901. From left: Chanute, Orville, Edward C. Huffaker and Wilbur. Wright photo

*PLATE 5 — Wilbur (left) and Orville fly glider No.2 as
a kite during July and August tests, Kitty Hawk, 1901.
Wright photo*

32

PLATE 6 — Dan Tate (left) and Edward C. Huffaker
launch glider, Kitty Hawk, 1901. Wright photo

PLATE 7 — Some flights ended like this. Orville with upended glider, Kitty Hawk, 1901. Wright photo

34

PLATE 8 — Wilbur at the end of a glide, Kitty Hawk, 1901. Longest glide was 389 feet. Wright photo

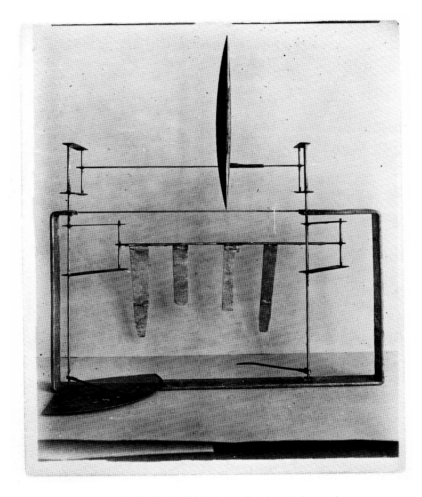

PLATE 9 — *The Wrights built this lift balance for the wind tunnel and tested their air foil designs from September 1901 to August 1902. Wright photo*

PHOTOGRAPHY, 1900-1905
In the photographic darkroom at home we pass moments of as thrilling interest as any in the field, when the image begins to appear on the plate and it is yet an open question whether we have a picture of a flying machine, or merely a patch of open sky.

Wilbur Wright, December, 1901

PLATE 10 — In glider No. 3, Orville turns in flight, Kitty Hawk, Oct. 10, 1902.
Wright photo

PLATE 11 — On top of Little Hill, Kitty Hawk, Oct. 10, 1902. From left: Octave Chanute, Orville and Wilbur Wright, Augustus M. Herring, George A. Spratt, Dan Tate. Wright photo

PLATE 12 — *Wilbur demonstrates turning ability of moveable, single rudder, Kitty Hawk, Oct. 24, 1902. Wright photo*

PLATE 13 — Charles Lamson's triple-wing glider at Pasadena, Cal., Sept. 8, 1902. Octave Chanute tested it unsuccessfully at Kitty Hawk the next month. Photo by Charles Lamson

PLATE 14 — Kitty Hawk, 1903 camp buildings in distance. 1902 glider with moveable double rudder pictured. Wright photo

PLATE 15 — Desolate, empty sands surround Wilbur, camp and airplane, Kitty Hawk, Nov. 24, 1903. Wright photo

44

PLATE 16 — Sleeping quarters at Kill Devil Hill camp, 1903. During sleepless night, Orville thought of the moveable rudder. In the morning Wilbur saw it could be combined with wing warping to control flight. Wright photo

1903

PLATE 17 — Distant view of camp buildings, Kitty Hawk, 1903 from wind-swept hill. Wright photo

DECEMBER 17, 1903
When we got up a wind of between 20 and 25 miles was blowing from the north . . . After running the engine and propellers a few minutes to get them in working order, I got on the machine at 10:35 for the first trial . . . On slipping the rope the machine lifted from the track just as it was entering on the fourth rail.

Orville Wright's Diary
Thursday, Dec. 17, 1903

PLATE 18 — *Famous first flight photo, Kitty Hawk, 10:35 a.m., Dec. 17, 1903. Before the 120-foot, 12-second flight, Orville positioned camera, instructed J.T. Daniels when to activate shutter. Orville developed negative later, in Dayton. Wright photo*

48

PLATE 19 — Flight 46, Simms Station near Dayton, Oct. 4, 1905. Second-longest flight of the year at 20.75 miles, 33 min., 17 sec. Wright photo

49

PLATE 20 — In 1905, the flights at Simms Station, the Wrights developed a practical machine that could take-off, fly, maneuver and land reliably. Wright photo

The Wrights did not fly between October, 1905 and May, 1908.
Because of unsuccessful negotiations with the U. S. Army, which
did not believe the brothers had a successful airplane to sell, and
due to the fear of industrial espionage, they refused to fly until
being offered a fair financial arrangement, by the government
or a private company.

Such an arrangement was concluded in Europe in 1908. The Army,
too, finally agreed to buy a Wright airplane, if it passed trials.

PHOTOGRAPHY, 1908-1911

The many professional and amateur photographers attending the public flying demonstrations in Europe and America made it unnecessary for the Wrights to take their own photographs. The prints of others provide a revealing overview of the technical and aesthetic developments in photography at that time. The smaller and more portable cameras introduced new and exciting visual possibilities into picture making. A looser and more spontaneous composition, combined with the dramatic cropping associated with a snapshot, became part of the photographic experience.

PLATE 21 — Ruins of 1903 camp and remains of 1902 glider, Kitty Hawk, 1908. Wright photo

LE MANS, FRANCE, 1908
In the second flight, I made an "eight" and landed at the starting point. The newspapers and the French aviators went wild with excitement. [Louis] Bleriot and [Leon] Delagrange were so excited they could scarcely speak, and [Henry] Kapferer could only gasp and could not talk at all. You would have almost died of laughter if you could have seen them.

Wilbur to Orville Wright
Aug. 15, 1908

56

PLATE 22 — Wilbur Wright adjusts motor, Le Mans, France, 1908. He made first public flight in August, astounding watchers and bringing on instant fame.

PLATE 23 — Orville went to Ft. Myer, Va. in September, 1908, to begin test flights for the U.S. Signal corps. This is a close-up of the airplane.

SEPTEMBER 17, 1908

Just after passing over the top of our building at a height which I estimate at 100 or 110 feet . . . I heard (or felt) a light tapping in the rear of the machine . . . I suppose it was not over two or three seconds from the time the first taps were heard, till two big thumps, which gave the machine a terrible shaking, showed that something had broken . . . Quick as a flash, the machine turned down in front and started straight for the ground . . . Lieutenant Selfridge up to this time had not uttered a word though he . . . turned once or twice to look into my face. But when the machine turned headfirst for the ground, he exclaimed "Oh! Oh!" in an almost inaudible voice.

Orville to Wilbur Wright
Nov. 14, 1908

60

PLATE 24 — The spectacular Ft. Myer demonstrations ended in a tragic accident in which Lt. T. E. Selfridge was killed and Orville badly injured, Sept. 17, 1908.

*PLATE 25 — Spectators at the Ft. Myers flying tests saw Orville make 10 flights in
10 days. He was airborne over six hours.*

PLATE 26 — Wright flyer and launching derrick, Pau, France, 1909. The device, which never failed in thousands of starts, provided extra safety margin as a weight catapulted plane on take-off.

*PLATE 27 — Pau, France, 1909. Working on launching track
made of $4.00 worth of 2 x 4's.*

64

PLATE 28 — *At Pau, Wilbur began training French pilots. Here he flies past as a man with a camera records scene. Photo by J. Callizo*

PLATE 29 — *Orville, still recovering from crash injuries, and sister Katharine joined Wilbur in Pau in January, 1909.*

PLATE 30 — *The Pau flights, such as this one over oxcarts, in France, 1909, attracted thousands, including European royalty.*

PLATE 31 — *Orville and Wilbur with Italian King Victor Emmanuel at Centocelle Field near Rome, April, 1909. Here the first motion pictures were taken from an airplane in flight.*

PLATE 32 — *The airplane in flight soon became a popular camera subject, this one in Italy, 1909.*

PLATE 33 — Orville and Wilbur with unidentified woman in this
"candid" shot, Italy, 1909.

PLATE 34 — An elegantly-dressed Orville with unidentified royalty in Italy in 1909.

PLATE 35 — Seems like everyone turned out to watch the flying demonstrations in Italy in 1909.

PLATE 36 — Orville went back to Ft. Myer, Va., for speed trials in July, 1909. The modified machine passed and U.S. Army bought its first plane.

PLATE 37 — *A crowd of 200,000, including these boys, watched Orville at a public exhibition at Tempelhof Field, Berlin, 1909.*

PLATE 38 — Crowds of children and adults watch the flights in Germany in 1909.

PLATE 39 — With such huge crowds, vantage points such as this fence, were at a premium. Germany, 1909.

76

PLATE 40 — Plane rests in hangar under guard, Germany, 1909.

PLATE 41 — These guards kept the curious a safe distance from hangar in Germany, 1909.

PLATE 42 — Eager hands roll the plane from hangar in this series of remarkable photos from Germany, 1909.

PLATE 43 — On the way to launching site, Germany, 1909.

PLATE 44 — *Airplane flies past small but intent group of watchers, Germany, 1909.*

PLATE 45 — *These public flights attracted a large crowd which came by foot, horse and auto, Germany, 1909.*

PLATE 46 — Airplane just after launching, Germany, 1909.

PLATE 47 — *Excited crowds running to get closer to the action at Tempelhof Field, Germany, 1909.*

PLATE 48 — *Orville established an altitude record of 902 feet on Sept. 30, 1909, on a flight such as this at Bornstedt, Germany.*

PLATE 49 — *While Orville flew in Germany, more than one-million people saw Wilbur fly at the Hudson-Fulton exhibition. Here, on Sept. 29, 1909 he flies around the Statue of Liberty in New York harbor.*

86

PLATE 50 — Wright Company flight school at Montgomery, Ala., May, 1910, on the site where Maxwell AFB now stands.

PLATE 51 — Airplane in flight over Dayton, Ohio, in 1910, labeled "fake" in Orville Wright's handwriting.

PLATE 52 — Orville and several Wright Co. exhibition pilots at International Aviation Tournament, Belmont Park, N.Y., 1910. Orville flew the Model R "Baby Grand" at speeds reaching 80 mph.

PLATE 53 — *Huge crowd jams Belmont Park grandstand. On Oct. 31, Wright flier Ralph Johnstone took a ''Baby Grand'' to a new altitude record of 9714 feet.*

CORNER OF SEWING DEPARTMENT

PLATE 54 — Ground was broken for a Dayton factory in January, 1910 and by May Orville was in charge of a flight school. Here Ida Holgrove works in the sewing department of the Wright Co. plant in 1911.

GENERAL MACHINE SHOP

PLATE 55 — Steinway and Harry Arnold work in machine shop at the Dayton factory in 1911.

BROTHERS

From the time we were little children, my brother Orville and myself lived together, worked together and, in fact, thought together. We usually owned all of our toys in common, talked over our thoughts and aspirations so that nearly everything that was done in our lives has been the result of conversations, suggestions and discussions between us.

Wilbur Wright, April 3, 1912

93

PLATE 56 — This is the scene which greeted Orville, brother Lorin and nephew Horace Wright when they returned to Kitty Hawk in October, 1911. In additional gliding experiments, Orville established a soaring record of 9 min., 45 secs. which stood for 10 years.

RON GEIBERT has been Assistant Professor of Art at Wright State University since 1981. A nationally exhibited artist, he has over 30 individual exhibitions to his credit and has participated in 70 group shows. His photographs are found in public and private collections including the Corcoran Gallery of Art, Washington, D.C.; the New Orleans Museum of Art; and the Ponderosa Collection. His photographs also appear in the publication, *Photography for Collectors, Volume II: The Midwest.*

TUCKER MALISHENKO served as the Aviation History specialist for the Wright State University Library Archives and Special Collections while a graduate assistant for the Department of History in 1982-1984. It was his special interest in the history of photography and his work in the Archives that prompted his idea for an exhibition of photographs from the Wright Brothers Collection.